At the time of
Picasso

THE FOUNDATIONS OF MODERN ART

PAPERBACK EDITION PRINTED IN 2008

© Aladdin Books Ltd 2002

Designed and produced by
Aladdin Books Ltd
2/3 Fitzroy Mews
London W1T 6DF

First published in 2002 by
Franklin Watts
338 Euston Road
London NW1 3BH

Franklin Watts Australia
Level 17/207 Kent Street
Sydney NSW 2000

Franklin Watts is a division of Hachette Children's Books

ISBN 978 0 7496 8128 9

*A catalogue record for this book
is available from the British Library.*

Dewey Classification: 759.06

Editors: Leen De Ridder, Kathy Gemmell, Liz White

Design: Flick, Book Design and Graphics

Picture Research: Brian Hunter Smart

Printed in Malaysia

Picture Credits
Abbreviations: l-left, r-right, b-bottom, t-top, c-centre, m-middle
Courtesy of AKG London
5tl, 10tl, 11tl, 12br, 40-41 — © Succession Picasso/DACS 2002.
6 both, 42-43 — © Succession H Matisse/DACS 2002. 7, 15br, 18tr, 21, 30tl, 32 both — © ADAGP, Paris and DACS,
London 2002. 22 both — © Succession Marcel Duchamp/ADAGP, Paris and DACS, London 2001. 24br, 28 both, 32bl,
38tl, 39b — © DACS 2002. 34br — © 2001 Mondrian/Holtzman Trust c/o Beeldrecht, Amsterdam, Holland and DACS,
London.
10bl, 16 both, 17bl, 19 both, 20 both, 24tl, 25t, 29, 30r, 31r, 34tl, 35br, 39bl, 41tr, 48.
Courtesy of Sotheby's
Front cover, 3, 44tl — © Succession Picasso/DACS 2002. 5b, 36 both — © DACS 2002. 24 both — © ADAGP, Paris and
DACS, London 2002. 42tl — © Succession H Matisse/DACS 2002. 25tr, 37t.
Courtesy of Museum of Modern Art, New York
11br — © Succession Picasso/DACS 2002.
Courtesy of Corbis
8tl — Geoffrey Clements/CORBIS. 8mr, 12tl, 13t, 14tl — Burstein Collection/CORBIS.
45br — © Succession Picasso/DACS 2002. 43ml, 47tr.
Other
4, 9, 14br, 46tr, 47b — Corel.
5tl, 23br, 46c — Select Pictures.

ART AROUND THE WORLD

At the time of
Picasso

Antony Mason

FRANKLIN WATTS
LONDON · SYDNEY

Contents

Introduction

In 1900, a new century dawned on an art world in a state of feverish turmoil, as a new generation of artists began to explore completely new directions in painting. They rejected the old idea of creating works that looked like the real world; photography could do that. Instead they took a fresh look at what art could do.

By abandoning traditional artistic skills and techniques, the artists freed their imaginations. They found that they could use colour and shapes to express emotions and inner thoughts, and to present new ways of looking at the world. To their satisfaction, this often caused outrage among art critics and the public, many of whom still wanted pretty landscapes or inspiring scenes from history to put on their walls.

The Fauves

Until about 1900, the French artist Henri Matisse (1869-1954) painted in the style of the Impressionists. In 1901, he met two younger artists, André Derain (1880-1954) and Maurice de Vlaminck (1876-1958). Together they worked at a new, vigorous way of painting, using bold brush strokes and slabs or blobs of unmixed colour. In the summer of 1905, Matisse and Derain painted together in the village of Collioure, in south-western France, and were thrilled by the rich, bright colours of the Mediterranean. Back in Paris, all three showed their work at the annual exhibition of new art, the Salon d'Automne.

Wild beasts

The critics and most of the public who saw these new works were shocked. They seemed rough and childlike. The colours were unrealistic and the drawing was very sketchy. One critic, Louis Vauxcelles, remarking on a sculpture in the middle of a room, said it was like a beautiful statue surrounded by *fauves* (wild beasts). This rather pleased the artists, who called themselves the Fauves. Their movement, Fauvism, became all the rage with young artists.

The Fauves rejected a host of old ideas about painting, and began applying colour in unexpected ways.

Above: Matisse worked on *Harmony in Red* (1908-9) over two years. Two paintings, *Harmony in Green* and *Harmony in Blue*, lie beneath the red that he finally settled on. The end result represents a movement away from the more turbulent brush strokes of earlier Fauve work.

Right: *Drying Sails* (1905), by André Derain, was painted during the summer of 1905. It was shown at the Salon d'Automne, where the term 'Fauvism' was coined.

Dabs of unrealistically bright, complementary colours fill Derain's *Drying Sails*. Matisse uses green in the face of his 1906 *Self-portrait*, and colour has become the main subject matter in his *Harmony in Red*, as reflected in the title.

The Fauves were not interested in drawing realistically. In *Harmony in Red*, Matisse has created flat colour, with virtually no perspective. The drawing – of the trees, for example – is stylised, and the patterning of the wallpaper and tablecloth has been given unreal emphasis. Instead of trying to show a realistic image, Matisse has rearranged colours and shapes in an effort to create a satisfactory composition, a 'harmony'. This reflects his great interest in the work of the Post-Impressionist Paul Cézanne (1839-1906), who had been working towards the same goal. The Fauvist movement ended in about 1908, but Matisse, Derain and Vlaminck continued working, developing their own styles, and they all lived on into the 1950s.

The Vienna Secession

By the late 19th century, young artists complained that the art world was dominated by the old-fashioned, traditional teaching methods of the academies, the official art schools. 'Academic art' represented mainstream taste, but young artists wanted something more inventive and energetic. Groups in Germany and Austria announced that they had officially seceded (broken away) from the mainstream, and set up Secession academies. The most famous movement of this kind was founded in Vienna in 1897.

Art and design

The Vienna Secession brought together not only artists and sculptors, but also architects and designers, who worked together to create the perfect designed environment. Gustav Klimt (1862-1918), a leading light in the movement, saw a close link between painting and decoration. Many of his most famous works were created as murals or wall panels. In fact, Klimt used a version of *The Kiss* in a mosaic frieze in the dining room of the ultra-modern Stoclet Palace in Brussels, designed by the Vienna Secession architect Josef Hoffmann.

Klimt's work has a highly sensual quality, and he painted a large number of nudes.

Houses with Drying Laundry (1917), by Schiele. His vigorous lines and rusty colours convey frenetic emotion and decay.

In part, this reflects new developments in the study of the subconscious mind by fellow Austrian, psychoanalyst Sigmund Freud. Klimt's gifted young friend Egon Schiele (1890-1918) also concentrated on studies of the human body. But there is a disturbing quality to Schiele's figures; the scrawny bodies with elongated limbs convey pent-up energy.

Klimt died as a result of a stroke in February 1918, aged 55. Schiele died eight months later, just three days after his wife. Both were victims of the flu epidemic that struck just after the end of the First World War (1914-1918). Schiele was 28 years old.

Klimt was known for his unusual painting clothes. He wore a long, ankle-length smock and looked like a monk. He was often seen in public in this outfit.

The Kiss (1907-8), by Klimt.

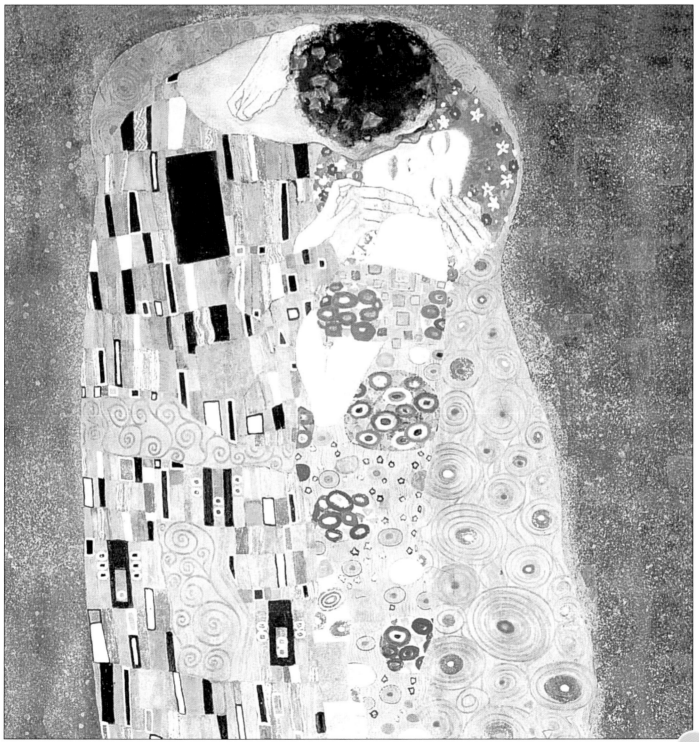

The Couple (1904), a work from Picasso's Blue Period.

Picasso and Cubism

After the Fauve exhibition in Paris in 1905, Matisse was celebrated as the leader of the avant-garde – those at the cutting edge of new art. But he had a rival. Living in Montmartre, the lively artists' quarter of Paris, was a young, brilliantly talented and ambitious artist from Spain, Pablo Picasso (1881-1973). Picasso saw the Fauve exhibition, noted the public attention that it attracted and was jealous. He realised that he needed to rethink his approach to painting, and within two years, he had created and launched Cubism. Picasso now took Matisse's place at the forefront of modern artistic taste.

Around the World
Africa

African artists have rarely attempted to create accurate and literal images of the world around them. Instead they express an interpretation of what they see. Often they may distort facial features, extend limbs and add colour. The result is a combination of imagination and artistic talent that can powerfully express emotions and qualities such as elegance, bravery, fearsomeness and humour. Until recently, African art was always closely connected to religious beliefs and rituals.

Painted wooden mask from northern Cameroon.

Above: Picasso's Family of Saltimbanques (1905) dates from his Rose Period. Off-stage acrobats and other circus performers became one of Picasso's favourite subjects.

Right: Picasso's Les Demoiselles d'Avignon (1907) was not shown until 1918. It portrays five prostitutes, whose bodies have been radically altered, simplified and jumbled up. The influence of African masks can be seen in the two faces on the right.

Influence on Western art

Artists like Picasso saw African art in museums. They were fascinated by the variety of the work, its range of imagination and its energy. Also, they envied its apparent freedom – freedom from the constraints of academic art and also in the choice of materials; African sculptors used not only wood and brass, but also shells, feathers, bone, raffia and bits of metal. They showed how it might be possible to take a fresh look at the world, and produce something original, new and exciting.

Blue and pink

Picasso first came to Paris in 1900, then returned in 1901, when a leading art dealer, Ambroise Vollard, mounted an exhibition of his work. Picasso moved between Paris and Barcelona before finally settling in Paris in 1904, aged 23. He had now developed his own distinct style, charging his work with brooding emotion and a sense of desolation. His paintings tended to be dominated by one colour. He progressed through a Blue Period (1900-4) to a slightly more cheerful Rose Period (1904-5).

Picasso built up his figures using thick paint and heavy outlines, and set them against a vague background. They are silent, uncommunicative figures, as if oppressed by the world around them. After 1905, Picasso pushed his art further towards experimentation. The result, two years later, was *Les Demoiselles d'Avignon* (*The Girls of Avignon*), a huge work, painted over months.

Portrait of the Artist (1916), by Gris.

The birth of Cubism

In 1907, Picasso met French painter Georges Braque (1882-1963). When they met again the following year, they realised that they both had the same vision for a new way of painting. So they began to work together. They tried to break up the visual world into geometric shapes – squares, triangles, cubes and cones. They also explored constructing an image as though it was being viewed from several angles at once. Again, the work of Paul Cézanne provided an inspiration; he had worked at ways of presenting reality as a composition of shapes. Picasso and Braque showed their work at the Salon d'Automne of 1908, where critic Louis Vauxcelles referred to their content as 'cubes' and 'cubic oddities'. Cubism was born, and went on to dominate the art scene until about 1914.

Mountaineers of art

At first, Picasso and Braque concentrated on still lifes, portraits and nudes, and tended to use dark colours. The effect was sombre and rather emotionless. In around 1911, they became more playful; Picasso added written words to his pictures, and then cuttings from newspapers and other printed material. From collage they started making three-dimensional 'constructions' from objects they had found, such as curtain tassels, spoons, tin cans and bits of skirting board, stuck together and painted. They called this new phase Synthetic Cubism.

Picasso and Braque enjoyed their close collaboration. Braque felt as if they were "roped together like mountaineers". Meanwhile, numerous other artists had taken up Cubism enthusiastically.

Carafe, Pitcher and Fruit Dish (1909), by Picasso. The carafe and other objects on the table have been broken up into cube-like shapes, injecting a new vibrancy into a simple still life.

Collage

The word 'collage' comes from the French *coller*, 'to stick'. It is a way of creating an image by cutting out pictures, patterns and words printed on paper and rearranging them to create a new image. People have been using printed cut-outs to make pictures for centuries, but the Cubists were the first serious artists to use collage in their work. At first they simply incorporated printed text, musical scores, tobacco packets, wallpaper, even chair-caning into their paintings. To many people in the art world, this was shocking; they expected paintings to consist entirely of work by the artist, not objects lifted from another source. Collage has become a widely used technique since then, and many artists have created complete pictures using collage.

One of the most successful new Cubists was Juan Gris (1887-1927), another Spanish painter, who lived in Paris and knew both Picasso and Braque. He applied to Cubism his particularly sensitive gifts of colour, shape and balance, and by 1912 was considered the third most important Cubist.

Gris continued painting in the Cubist style until he died, long after Picasso had moved onto new ideas. Picasso constantly changed his style during his long life, at each phase opening up new paths which other artists followed. For him, Cubism ended with the First World War.

New Concepts in Sculpture

During his Cubist period, Picasso created many inventive sculptures. Some were made from wood, and were clearly inspired by the art of Africa and the islands of the South Pacific. Some were made of objects he had found, stuck together and painted. He was constantly playing with new ideas and new ways to create art. He was not alone in such experimentation. At the same time, also living in Montmartre, were the Italian Amedeo Modigliani (1884-1920) and the Romanian Constantin Brancusi (1876-1957). Both took sculpture in new directions.

A Student, a typical portrait by Modigliani, showing the close parallels with his sculpture.

Painter and sculptor

Modigliani is known primarily as a painter. But after he met Brancusi in 1909, he turned exclusively to sculpture for five years. After the outbreak of the First World War in 1914, he was unable to obtain marble, and so returned to painting. He died of tuberculosis not long after the war ended, aged only 35. His subject matter was almost always the same: women. He painted and sculpted their images in a style that is instantly recognisable, with elongated heads and limbs and simplified features. Both Modigliani's paintings and sculptures show the influence of African masks on his work.

The young sculptors of the avant-garde, like Brancusi, were highly critical of the sculpture that appeared in public places in their day. Most of these were bronze figures that commemorated a politician or general, usually modelled in a stylised, unimaginative way designed to flatter and impress.

War memorials

After the First World War, countless memorials to the dead were erected across Europe. Most are very ordinary, impressive only in the pitifully long lists of names. A famous exception is the *Royal Artillery Memorial*, by British sculptor C. Sargeant Jagger (1885-1934), himself wounded in the war. War-weary bronze soldiers stand beside a stone gun, expressing the unglamorous hard work and pain of war. It was criticised at the time for not showing a more glorious image.

The Royal Artillery Memorial (1921-25), Hyde Park Corner, London, by C. Sargeant Jagger.

Brancusi was a gifted sculptor who could have worked with Rodin, the greatest French sculptor of his day, who was famous for his highly realistic human figures. Instead, Brancusi chose to follow his own unique path. Working in stone, metal and wood, he simplified forms to their bare essentials – often smooth, rounded shapes. It was as though he was sculpting not how things looked, but the idea of them, or, as he put it, "the essence of things". Brancusi became an international celebrity during his lifetime, and his innovative approach was a major influence in the development of 20th-century sculpture.

Brancusi's sculpture Bird in Space (1927) was such a simple shape that US Customs officials refused to believe it was a sculpture – they said it was a lump of raw metal.

Sleeping Muse (c.1906-10), by Brancusi. Like Modigliani, Brancusi was strongly influenced by African art. The Muses were the Greek goddesses who inspired artists.

Expressionism
Die Brücke

While the Fauves were experimenting with colour in France, a similar movement began in Germany. In Dresden in 1905, Ernst Ludwig Kirchner (1880-1938) and Karl Schmidt-Rottluff (1884-1976) formed a group called Die Brücke (The Bridge) – the bridge to the future of art. For a time, they were joined by Emil Nolde (1867-1956). Their paintings display a deliberately crude approach to drawing and colouring, and show startling aggression and emotion. This emotion is expressed not only in the subject matter, but also in the way the paint has been applied. In about 1911, this kind of painting was labelled Expressionism.

Call to action

The Die Brücke artists had much in common with the Fauves; they used bright colour, rapid brush strokes and crude drawing. Like their colleagues in France, they were influenced by sculpture from Africa and the South Pacific. But the raw emotional content of Die Brücke's works make the Fauves seem quite tame and happy in comparison.

In style and brushwork, Die Brücke took its lead from Post-Impressionists, such as van Gogh, Gauguin and Ensor, but the emotional content could be traced back to works like *The Scream* (1893), by the Norwegian artist Edvard Munch (1863-1944). They found that woodcut prints could also express the brutal feelings that they wanted to convey.

Nolde's Crucifixion (1912) shows the influence of German medieval art, such as the work of Matthias Grünewald and Lucas Cranach. Nolde was himself deeply religious.

16

Kirchner expressed the rebellious nature of the Die Brücke movement when he tried to describe its intentions. Like many arts manifestos of the era, his writing reads like a call to revolution: "We call together all youth... We want to create for ourselves the freedom of life and action against the well-established older forces." Kirchner's work often reflects a burning anger against the ills of society.

Nolde's paintings are more mystical, often religious, but filled with urgent anxiety or frenetic movement. His landscapes convey his fascination with the forces of nature.

Nolde led a rather isolated life, and stayed with Die Brücke for only a year (1906-07).

In 1911, Kirchner, Schmidt-Rottluff and others in the group moved to Berlin. Kirchner wrote a history of Die Brücke in 1913, but this opened up disagreements within the group and it fell apart. In the 1930s, Kirchner's work was condemned by the Nazis and confiscated. Already prone to depression, he committed suicide in 1938.

Around the World
New Guinea

In his history of Die Brücke, Kirchner explained how the art of the South Pacific islands had a major impact on the group. The masks of New Guinea made a particularly strong impression. Nolde even went to New Guinea in 1913-14 to gain first-hand experience of these artefacts.

Art of the ancestors

In the past, all art in New Guinea had religious significance. This included carved decorations on spoons and bowls and on the bows of fishing boats. The images were connected to the protecting gods and the spirits of the ancestors. Many elaborate masks were created for a particular ritual, then destroyed. So they were often constructed from materials that would not last, such as mud and grasses or dough made out of vegetable matter, and painted with natural dyes. Only the more solid (often less inventive) pieces reached Western museums.

Carved wooden image of a spirit figure, from the Sepik River region of northern New Guinea.

Der Blaue Reiter

In 1911, another set of Expressionists formed a group in Munich, Germany. The founding artists were Franz Marc (1880-1916), August Macke (1887-1914) and Russian-born Wassily Kandinsky (1866-1944). They called themselves Der Blaue Reiter (The Blue Rider), apparently simply because they all liked the colour blue, and because Marc liked to paint horses and Kandinsky liked to paint riders. It was also the name of a painting by Kandinsky. Other members of the group included Swiss-born Paul Klee (1879-1940).

Der Blaue Reiter's aim to create a radically new kind of art echoes Die Brücke's intention of making a complete break with the past.

Treatises and Manifestos

Art movements became very self-conscious in the early 20th century. New movements strived to be awarded a catchy label ending in *-ism*, such as Fauvism, Cubism or Expressionism. To explain their aims, artists would write and publish texts. Some were in the form of treatises – careful analyses of the principles, leading to a conclusion. Kandinsky wrote a treatise called *On the Spiritual in Art* in 1911. It explored how philosophy, religion, music and colour could create harmonies that lead to 'spiritual awakening', and how this could be achieved in art. This helped to explain the aims of Der Blaue Reiter, as too did the *Almanak*, published by Kandinsky and Marc the following year.

Other artists wrote a more forceful statement of their intentions, called a manifesto. The language was less analytical – more like a politician's speech. A manifesto was designed to win support by appealing to emotions and stirring up enthusiasm.

Book cover design (1911), in ink and watercolour, by Kandinsky, for Der Blaue Reiter Almanak. The book contained a collection of texts and illustrations about non-Western cultures that were deemed to possess the power of 'spiritual awakening'.

Marc summed this up by saying, "We must be bold and turn our backs upon everything that until now good Europeans like ourselves thought precious and indispensable."

But Der Blaue Reiter's approach to painting was less aggressive and more softly poetic than Die Brücke's. The group's work also attracted a far wider circle of followers – 43 artists took part in their first exhibition in 1911. Their exhibition in Munich in 1912 also included works by Die Brücke artists Nolde and Kirchner, and by Picasso and Braque.

Spiritual art

Der Blaue Reiter's work was considered highly original at the time, mainly because of its serious aim to create a new, spiritual kind of art. The artists wanted their paintings to express feelings, not reality, so they tried to abandon any naturalistic representation of reality. They did this by using non-naturalistic colours and by breaking up their compositions into blocks that recall Cubist work. They hoped to achieve a 'spiritual awakening' through art. To help them find a path to this goal, they explored naive and ethnic art, and also children's painting.

Marc's work in particular has a mystical quality, reflecting his religious convictions.

The Jumping Horse (1912), by Marc. Disgusted by his fellow human beings, Marc placed animals on a higher spiritual plane. Horses were one of his favourite subjects, here seen in a composition clearly influenced by Cubism.

He tended to paint subjects from nature, especially animals, using soft, glowing colours. Macke's work is poetic, personal and mysterious. Kandinsky carried out some of the first experiments in completely abstract art.

Like Die Brücke, Der Blaue Reiter came to a halt with the outbreak of the First World War. Marc and Macke joined the army; Macke was killed in 1914, aged 27; Marc was killed in 1916, aged 26.

Mirror Image in a Shop Window (1913), by Macke. A small work in ink, about the size of an A4 sheet of paper, it has the intimate, personal quality of much of Macke's work.

Der Blaue Reiter was the first movement to take an interest in children's art. As Macke wrote, children "express themselves directly from their innermost feelings".

The Futurists

The Futurists were a group of Italian artists and writers who developed an enthusiasm for everything modern, and a burning desire to steer society towards a bright, modern future. They gloried in machines, the speed of the car, the bustle of cities and the triumphs of factories. They hated dreamy symbolism, and demanded steely, focused logic in its place. They wanted to kick the world out of its slumber and start afresh. In art, this meant throwing out all conventions and traditions of the past.

Machine-age art

The Italian poet Filippo Tommaso Marinetti published the first *Futurist Manifesto* in Paris in 1909. He set out the Futurists' way of thinking in a provocative manner, with sentiments like, "A screaming automobile that seems to run like a machine gun is more beautiful than the *Victory of Samothrace*" (a masterpiece of ancient Greek sculpture).

The main Futurist artists, Giacomo Balla (1871-1958) and Umberto Boccioni (1882-1916), followed this with manifestos about Futurist painting and sculpture. They proposed using all means available to create a new kind of art. Borrowing from artistic styles such as Pointillism (which they called Divisionism) and Cubism, they painted visions of a future world full of machines, factories, speed and power.

Multiple-exposure painting

Balla is best known for his witty paintings of motion, like *Girl Running on a Balcony* and *Dynamism of a Dog on a Leash* (1912), which shows a dachshund walking beside its owner, with its legs and tail in a blur of about eight different positions. We are used to this technique now (often used in comic strips), but it was a new idea in 1912. The technique was inspired by multiple-exposure photography, where photographers used a series of cameras to take photos in rapid sequence, in order to capture movement. Balla combined these in one image.

The great clash

Launched in Paris when Cubism was all the rage, Futurism offered a radically different vision. Early Cubism was contemplative and silent, rather sombre and static. Futurism was bright and brash, noisy and full of movement.

Futurism also concerned more than just art; its vision encompassed all aspects of modern life. In a more sinister vein, many of the Futurists looked forward to a mighty war, hoping to see a great clash of nations with modern weapons, which would sweep out the past and clear the way for a modern future. War came in 1914, but in fact effectively put an end to Futurism. Boccioni joined the Italian army and was killed in an accident. In the 1920s and 1930s, Futurism was adopted by the Italian Fascists. This gave the movement a bad name, from which it has never really recovered.

The Futurists believed that all objects in the world have a character, vitality and energy of their own. These are revealed in the 'force lines' expressed in their shape.

Far left: In his Factories in Porta Roma (1909), Boccioni attempts to prettify industrial production, filling a factory scene with colour and sunlight.

Left: Girl Running on a Balcony (1912), by Balla.

Both of these paintings use broken dots of unmixed colour. Known as Divisionism, this was a favourite technique of the Futurists in the early years. The dotting effect makes the colour more vibrant, and enhances the sense of movement.

Duchamp

The French artist Marcel Duchamp (1887-1968) came to public attention in 1913, when his ground-breaking Cubist-Futurist work (below) was shown at the influential Armory Show in New York – a showcase of international contemporary art. It was greeted with a mixture of acclaim and horror by the critics and the general public. That same year, he produced the first of his 'ready-mades' – ordinary objects which he said were art simply because he declared them to be so. Much of late 20th-century art can be traced back to this controversial gesture.

The art of selection

Duchamp came from a family of artists, and studied painting part-time while working as a librarian in Paris. He kept a close eye on current trends in art, and adopted aspects of Fauvism and then Cubism, as seen in his painting *Sonata*.

The art movements of the day, such as Cubism, Expressionism and Futurism, wanted to erase all preconceived, historic notions about art. Duchamp's ready-mades took a leap along this line of logic. If, say, the Cubists could make sculptures out of found objects, then what was art? He decided that art was just a question of selection and presentation. His early ready-mades included *Bicycle Wheel* (1913), a real bicycle wheel mounted on a wooden stool. He went even further with *Fountain* (1917), a men's porcelain urinal which he signed with the name R. Mutt.

Nude Descending a Staircase No. 2 (1912), by Duchamp. He painted very little after this, but concentrated on assemblies of objects.

After *Nude Descending a Staircase*, the world paid little attention to Duchamp's work. But in the 1960s, he was acclaimed as one of the great masters of the 20th century.

Fountain was rejected for a show by New York's Society of Independent Artists, but someone (probably Duchamp himself) wrote in its defence, "Whether Mr Mutt with his own hands made the fountain or not has no importance. He CHOSE it." Thus the art was not in the object itself, but in the idea that it provoked.

Meanwhile, Duchamp worked on *The Bride Stripped Bare by Her Bachelors, Even* (also known as *The Large Glass*) for over eight years (1915-23). Made of oil paint and lead foil, mounted on glass so that it can be seen from both sides, it has been the subject of endless speculation. Duchamp declared, "There is no solution, because there is no problem."

After 1942, he worked secretly on an installation of a room, viewed through two peepholes.

Around the World
Spain

In the years before the First World War, one of the world's most extraordinary and original architects was making a name for himself. Antoní Gaudí (1852-1926) created buildings inspired by nature – by the sea, the sun, shells and maize cobs. His apartments and houses in Barcelona were full of curving walls and extravagant shapes, and decorated with colourful tiles.

Living architecture

Gaudí's work contains many of the curvaceous qualities of Art Nouveau, the design style that emerged in the 1890s. In 1883, he was put in charge of designing a church in Barcelona called the Sagrada Familia, and after 1916 he worked on nothing else. It has a cluster of spindly towers decorated as if with dribbled sand. It remains unfinished, but building continues.

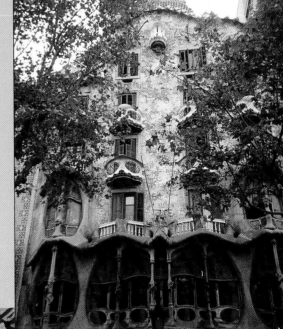

Casa Batlló, Barcelona, an apartment block designed by Gaudí and built in 1905-7.

The Birth of Abstract Art

One day in 1910, the Russian-born artist Wassily Kandinsky, a founder member of the Expressionist group Der Blaue Reiter, walked into his studio and was stunned by what he saw. "Suddenly my eyes fell upon an indescribably beautiful picture that was saturated with an inner glow... it was one of my own paintings leaning on its side against the wall." This experience inspired him to work on a series of paintings that did not represent anything in the real world – they were just colours and shapes arranged in the composition. They were, in a word, 'abstract'.

The poetry of colour

Whether Kandinsky was the first artist in the modern era to pursue abstract painting as an art form is not clear. Several other painters of the time were thinking along the same lines, including the American Arthur Dove (1880-1946). But Kandinsky was at the centre of an influential art movement, and soon a number of artists were exploring the possibilities of abstract art.

Composition (c.1915-17), by Kandinsky.
He believed that art should be a true expression of inner feelings, and saw abstract art as a perfect vehicle to achieve this.

In France a group of artists came together in 1911 to attempt to create a brighter, more poetic form of Cubism. The movement was labelled Orphism, or Orphic Cubism, after Orpheus, a lyre player in Greek mythology.

Circular Forms: Sun No. 3 (1912-13), by Delaunay.

Among this group were Robert Delaunay (1885-1941) and František Kupka (1871-1957), who tried to find a connection between abstract art and music. Orphism lasted only until 1914, but had a big impact on other movements, including Der Blaue Reiter.

Meanwhile, two American painters, Stanton Macdonald-Wright (1890-1973) and Morgan Russell (1886-1953), formed the Synchromism movement ('colours together'). They also claimed to be the original pioneers of abstract art.

Around the World
South Sea Islands

The idea of creating pictures out of non-representational shapes was not new – decorative patterns have been made since ancient times. Delicate, geometric patterns decorate a traditional kind of felt-like cloth on the South Pacific islands of Fiji, Tonga and Samoa. The cloth is called tapa, and is used for clothing, ceremonial carpets, bedcovers and wall hangings.

Printing and painting

To make the cloth, thin strips of bark are beaten together to form a thin sheet. The designs may first be laid out on a separate palm-frond mat, over which the cloth is laid. Brown stain is then rubbed on to pick up the pattern underneath. The patterns are embellished with paint.

Tapa (bark cloth) designs, from Tonga.

Constructivism and Suprematism

Abstract art also caught on in Russia. Russia was in a state of political turmoil, deeply involved in the First World War, and heading towards the chaos and massive upheavals of the Communist Revolution of 1917. Radical artists such as Vladimir Tatlin (1885-1953) saw abstract art as a way of expressing the hopes and aspirations of the industrial workers. He believed that ordinary people needed a new, modern type of art with no links to the past.

Constructing art

Tatlin began his career as a painter, but in 1914 he met Picasso and was inspired to try to create abstract, Cubist structures. He was joined by abstract painter Alexander Rodchenko (1891-1956), and by sculptors Naum Gabo (1890-1977) and his brother Antoine Pevsner (1886-1962). Their aim was to 'construct' art from abstract forms, and the movement was called Constructivism.

At the same time, Russian painter Kasimir Malevich (1878-1935) developed a new style of abstract painting, Suprematism, which had no reference to the natural world. He hoped to reveal the supremacy of artistic sensitivity. In 1918, he made a series of paintings consisting of a white square on a white background.

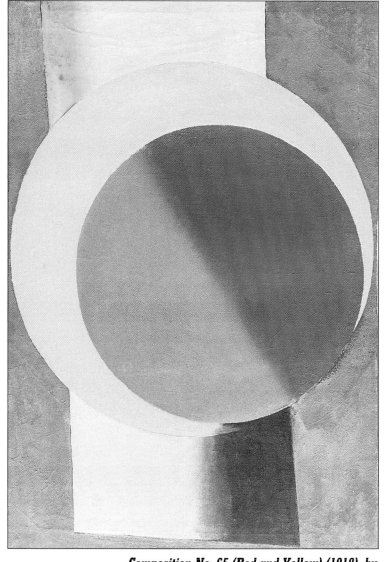

Composition No. 65 (Red and Yellow) (1918), by Rodchenko. He used a ruler and compass to create these tidy geometric shapes.

26

Suprematist Composition (1915), by Malevich.

The Suprematists and the Constructivists argued about the function of art. The Suprematists felt that art was a goal in itself, but the Constructivists believed that art should serve more practical, social purposes.

After the Revolution, Tatlin tried to turn Constructivism into a blend of art and architecture. His most ambitious project was the *Monument to the Third International* of 1921, a vast spiralling iron and glass structure with revolving exhibition and congress halls. However, only a model of the structure was ever built. In the 1920s, Tatlin and Rodchenko increasingly concentrated on industrial design.

It is not always clear which way up Malevich's paintings go. Photographs of early exhibitions show the same paintings hung with a different edge at the top.

By this time, the Soviet authorities had decided to support a more popular and realistic kind of art, called Social Realism, which depicted heroic workers. Constructivism fell from favour, and Pevsner and Gabo, who had always been less convinced of the social role of art, fled abroad. The others stayed on in relative obscurity, although Rodchenko became a celebrated photographer.

Dada

The First World War had a deep impact on Europe. Not only were many millions of people killed and wounded, but there was also a feeling that the way of life that preceded the war was responsible for causing it. For many artists and writers in the avant-garde, this called for a new look at the world, and a radical change in attitudes. One group decided that the best response was to stop taking everything so seriously, and to poke fun at art. The result was the madcap antics of a movement called Dada.

Fun and nonsense

Dada in fact began during the war in Zürich, in neutral Switzerland, where a number of artists, writers and musicians had taken refuge. Disillusioned with politics and the art world, they started to challenge everything, largely by making fun of it. They produced a number of art objects and events, which they claimed had no meaning at all. The name Dada is appropriately baffling: it is a child's word for a hobby horse, chosen apparently at random.

The Cabaret Voltaire, founded in Zürich in 1916, established Dada first as a literary movement. Writers produced poems and sketches of complete gibberish, and music made up of peculiar noises, or played on kitchen utensils. One of the group was the French artist and sculptor Jean Arp (1886-1966), who made collages of casually dropped paper.

Merz Drawing 297 (Yellow) (1921), by Schwitters. Schwitters's 'Merz' collages were made up of pieces of rubbish – cigarette packets, bus tickets, wallpaper and, in this case, discarded pieces of lace.

Dada spread to other cities after the war. Arp formed a Dada group in Cologne, Germany, with Max Ernst (1891-1976), who made a study of the art of mental patients. Kurt Schwitters (1887-1948) was the only member of a group in Hanover. A New York group was formed by Duchamp, the American Man Ray (1890-1977) and Francis Picabia (1879-1953), who later took the movement to Barcelona and Paris.

The Dada movement had run out of steam by about 1922, but it had a lasting influence. It celebrated an unrestrained approach to art and permitted the art world to have fun.

Photomontage

The technique known as photomontage was pioneered in Berlin by John Heartfield (1891-1968) and Hannah Höch (1889-1987). It is effectively a kind of collage using photographs, often taken from magazines. The technique suited Dada well. Surprising and sometimes shocking pictures could be created easily by mixing images that would not normally be seen together. Both Heartfield and Höch continued using photomontage throughout their careers. Their work often had a political edge. Photomontage had a considerable influence on various art movements throughout the 20th century.

The opening of the First International Dada Fair, in 1920, which took place in a bookshop in Berlin. The poster on the left reads, "Take Dada seriously, it's worth it!"

At a famous Dada exhibition in 1920, organised by Max Ernst, visitors entered via the toilets and were given axes so they could destroy the exhibits if they wished.

Surrealism

Dada was essentially an anti-art gesture, poking fun at the art world. "A true Dadaist is against [even] Dada", the saying went. Serious artists found it hard to sustain this negative approach to art. Many of them turned to Surrealism, which proposed a more constructive, well-argued case for a new approach to art and literature. Surrealism is often said to concern the world of dreams. But that is only part of it. It was an exploration of the subconscious world – all the functions of the mind beyond rational thought, such as instinct and free association.

Inner worlds

Much of the Surrealists' work is bizarre, but there was some serious thinking behind the movement. The Surrealists believed that the realm of the subconscious mind was more powerful and more reliable than rational thought, on which everyday life was supposed to be based. They believed that the subconscious mind held the key to a more truthful and superior reality – a sur-reality.

Surrealism was launched in Paris in 1924, when the French poet André Breton published the first *Surrealist Manifesto*. Like Dada, in the first instance it was seen mainly as a literary movement. But it struck a chord with many of the Dada artists, such as Man Ray, Max Ernst and Jean Arp, who applied Surrealism to the visual arts.

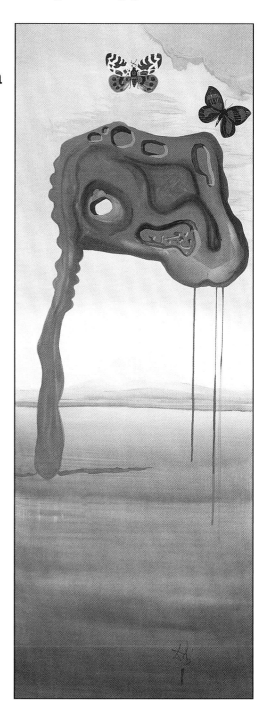

Surrealist Landscape (c.1968), by Dalí.
The central feature is typically baffling.

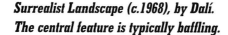

Around the World
Mexico

The Surrealists had a special fondness for Mexico, which they declared the most surreal of all countries. Much of the work of Mexico's most famous female artist, Frida Kahlo (1907-54), is tinged with Surrealism. Her paintings are often autobiographical, and contain disturbing symbols of her troubled private life, her emotional turmoil and physical pain.

The pain within

When she was 18, Kahlo was badly injured in a tram accident, which left her in physical pain for the rest of her life. In 1928, she married Diego Rivera (1886-1957), who was Mexico's best-known artist. It was the beginning of a stormy on-off relationship, which became the subject of many of her paintings. The combination of her inner thoughts and influences from naive Mexican folk art gives her work a distinctly surreal effect. Although Surrealists admired her, she never claimed to be part of the movement.

Self-portrait with Little Monkeys (1945), by Kahlo. This was one of a number of self-portraits featuring a monkey at her shoulder.

The best-known Surrealist painters developed their own distinct personal artistic styles. The Belgian René Magritte (1898-1967) painted very detailed, technically accomplished images in a realistic manner, but they always contain some absurdity.

The Spanish painter Salvador Dalí (1904-89) is famous for his desert landscapes, painted with great precision, but with strange objects in them, such as melting watches or dead trees.

In 1936, Dalí gave a lecture at an exhibition dressed in a diver's outfit. The helmet became stuck, and he had to be rescued from suffocation.

31

Chagall and de Chirico

Strange, dreamlike qualities are found in the work of two other major painters of the 20th century. Marc Chagall (1887-1985) was born in Russia, but lived most of his long life in France, dying at the age of 97. His paintings express a highly autobiographical world that incorporates Jewish folklore, Bible stories and personal memories, painted in a fairy-tale style. The Italian Giorgio de Chirico (1888-1978) is best known for his strangely haunting street scenes, filled with an eerie mixture of silence, calm and unease. Both artists, however, declared that they were not Surrealists.

Memories

Chagall was brought up in the Jewish community of Vitebsk, in western Russia (now Belarus). He studied art in St Petersburg, then in 1910 went to live in Paris for four years. Here he came into contact with avant-garde movements of the day – Cubism, Orphism and the pioneers of abstract art. In Berlin in 1914, he saw the work of the German Expressionists. While running an art academy in Vitebsk, he worked alongside Kasimir Malevich, but disagreed strongly with his approach to art. In 1923 he returned to France, where, with the Italian Modigliani and other non-French artists, he formed a group known as the School of Paris. They painted in a mainly realistic style sometimes known as Poetic Expressionism.

The Walk (1917), by Chagall, a self-portrait with his new wife. The elements of fantasy are typical of Chagall's work.

Chagall now also developed his career as a book illustrator and printmaker. He stayed in France for the rest of his life, except for a seven-year spell in the USA, after fleeing from the German occupation of France in 1941 during the Second World War.

Despite Chagall's contacts with so many key movements of contemporary art, his style remained utterly individual.

The magic of objects

De Chirico was born in Greece, and trained in Athens, Florence and Munich. He developed a distinctive style – images of empty streets and squares containing objects such as tailors' dummies and gloves, all painted in drained colours. He tried to create a feeling of mystery and hallucination, and Picasso and other members of the avant-garde were impressed.

While recovering from a nervous breakdown, de Chirico formulated his ideas into a theory of 'Metaphysical Painting'. This had a major impact on the emerging Surrealists. But in the late 1920s, he began to adopt a more traditional style of painting, which the Surrealists did not appreciate.

The Surrealists loved de Chirico's early work, but criticised his paintings of the late 1920s. De Chirico was furious, and denied that he had painted the early work at all.

The Great Metaphysician (1916), by de Chirico. Metaphysics is the philosophical study that deals with the fundamental questions of being and knowledge. De Chirico used the term to describe the magical quality of objects, which, he claimed, could be exposed by placing them out of context. Here they combine to form the body of a piece of Classical sculpture – a feature of many of his works, echoing his background in Italy and Greece.

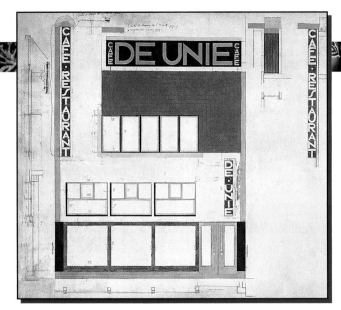

Mondrian and De Stijl

The Dutch artist Piet Mondrian (1872-1944) lived in Paris in the years leading up to the First World War. He was intrigued by Cubism, and adopted its style in his painting. Gradually his work became more and more abstract. After returning to The Netherlands at the outbreak of the First World War, he came to the conclusion that Cubism had not gone nearly far enough. In 1917, he started to break up his work into entirely abstract compositions of horizontal and vertical lines and rectangles, painted in black and white (and sometimes grey) together with primary colours.

Art and architecture

Mondrian's work was revolutionary. No one had produced abstract paintings that were quite so simple, geometric and mathematical. For their success, these works depended entirely on the artist's judgement about spacing and colours.

During the early 20th century, many artists were fascinated by the connection between art and architecture. A group of Dutch artists and designers wondered how Mondrian's work could be converted into architecture and interior design. They included the painter Theo van Doesburg (1883-1931), and architects Gerrit Rietveld (1888-1964) and J.J.P. Oud (1890-1963). With Mondrian, they formed a design group and produced a magazine, both called De Stijl (The Style).

Composition in Yellow, Red, Black, Blue and Grey (1920), by Mondrian. This is a typical title for Mondrian's early abstract work. He wanted to show that it contained no reference to anything outside the painting.

De Stijl had a major influence on design and architecture, in particular through the famous German architecture school called the Bauhaus. Many leading avant-garde artists taught art at the school, including Kandinsky, Klee, Gabo and van Doesburg.

Mondrian had a strong belief in his theories, and fell out with other members of De Stijl over the use of diagonal lines. Only towards the end of his life did he soften his style and introduce more colours into his work.

Mondrian called his style Nieuwe Beelding (new image-making), which was translated as 'Neo-Plasticism'. He believed that art should be abstract, with no reference to the natural world. By restricting the work to lines and rectangles of primary colours, he hoped to minimise any expression of the artist's individuality. In so doing, he claimed artists could reveal a sense of universal harmony. Mondrian first wrote about this theory in a series of articles called 'Neo-Plasticism in Pictorial Art', published in *De Stijl* magazine in 1917-18.

Around the World
France

De Stijl and the Bauhaus produced ultra-modern designs in which all decoration has been stripped away. This austere style had only limited public appeal. More popular was an elaborate design style that later became known as Art Deco, after the 1925 Exposition Internationale des Arts Décoratifs et Industrielles Modernes, the exhibition in Paris where it first made an impact.

Art Deco

In the 1920s, Art Deco was considered a glitzy, glamorous style, with sharp angles and flashy surfaces of chrome. It included the exotic influences of Aztec design and the ancient Egyptian treasure of Tutankhamun. Initially, Art Deco style was used by specialist designers and furniture makers working for wealthy clients, or to decorate cinemas. By the 1930s, the style had been widely adopted for factory-produced goods, such as mirrors, wall lamps, hairbrushes and new electrical appliances.

Art Deco electric clock, made in Paris in 1927.

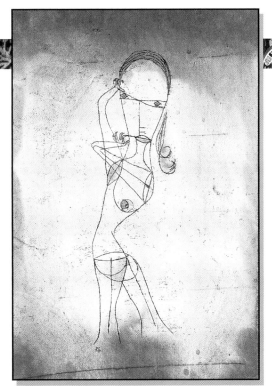

Klee and Miró

The German-Swiss painter Paul Klee (1879-1940) was a member of the German Expressionist group Der Blaue Reiter. The Spanish painter Joan Miró (1893-1983) was closely associated with the Surrealists and André Breton called him "the most Surrealist of all". Yet both these artists were too individual to fit readily into any category. Many of their paintings are delightfully filled with charm, humour and personality. Often looking like doodles, they fall somewhere between abstract art and Surrealism.

Colour and line

Klee trained at the Munich Academy, where he met the members of Der Blaue Reiter. He exhibited with them in 1912. Up until 1914, he worked mainly in black and white, but then he travelled to Tunisia. Inspired by the light and colours of North Africa, he underwent an almost mystical conversion to colour. This is seen particularly in a patchwork effect he used in many of his paintings.

The Birth of the Kite (1927), by Klee. Neither entirely abstract nor representational, this painting appears to depict a private world of thought and imagination, like so many of Klee's pieces.

With a major exhibition of his work in Munich in 1919, Klee shot to international fame. This run of luck came to a close with the rise of the Nazis, who hated avant-garde art. He moved to Switzerland and became depressed and ill. In his final years his work became noticeably more bleak.

Miró's design for the cover of the catalogue for the Joan Miró Prize.

Spontaneous art

Born and trained in Barcelona, Miró first
went to Paris in 1919, where he came into
contact with all the early art movements of
the 20th century, from Fauvism to Dada. He
became friends with fellow Spaniard
Picasso. But the most important inspiration
for his work was Surrealism, and he joined
the movement at its inception in 1924. In
keeping with Surrealist ideals, almost all his
work concerns the release of images from
the subconscious mind. They often look like
spontaneous doodles, part abstract, part
animal. As he explained, "I begin painting
and as I paint the picture begins to assert
itself, or suggest itself, under my brush."
Klee's work became an important influence
for Miró in the late 1920s.

Klee produced a vast
quantity of work – a total of
nearly 8,000 paintings and drawings
– in the course of his lifetime.
Most of it is on a small scale.

Miró used to return to Spain each year to
spend summer on the family farm, but during
the Spanish Civil War (1936-39) he was forced
to stay in Paris. His work now lost much of its
humour and became more sombre. In 1940, the
Germans occupied Paris, and Miró fled to the
Spanish island of Majorca. As his international
fame grew after the war, he broadened his
work to include pottery, sculpture, large murals
for public places and stained glass.

War in the Trenches (1932), by Dix.

Commenting on Society

The 1920s and 1930s were harrowing times in Europe. Germany, devastated by the First World War, was condemned to poverty. In politics, communists and socialists clashed violently with the right-wing forces of fascism. The Soviet Union was still struggling to find stability after the Revolution of 1917. In the 1930s, the Nazis came to power in Germany, and Spain erupted into vicious civil war. Many artists vented their anguish, rage and dismay in their art.

Around the World
The Soviet Union

After 1917, the government of the new Soviet Union took control of all aspects of life, including art. Government officials had little time for avant-garde art, which they found too remote from the tastes of the common people.

Poster art

Instead, the Soviet authorities promoted a more realistic form of art, called Social Realism. It was used for pro-government propaganda. Powerful images showed how ordinary people could fight the enemies of communism through courage, hard work and obedience to the cause.

Propaganda poster (1943), promoting civil defence against enemy air raids.

Savaging the rich

German artists produced some of the most biting social criticism. The most prominent among them were George Grosz (1893-1957) and Otto Dix (1891-1969). Using caricature and a wide range of painting techniques, they poured scorn on the German government, middle-class values and the greed and hypocrisy of city life. In 1925, they formed a movement called Neue Sachlichkeit (New Objectivity), an obscure title referring to their style of painting, which was based on realism. This was in contrast to most of the other avant-garde trends of the day, which were concerned with abstract art and the workings of the mind.

Dix was haunted by the horror of war and the long-term suffering that it caused, and these themes stayed with him through the 1920s and 1930s. His dislike of all things military drew him into conflict with the Nazis in the 1930s, and he was forced into semi-retirement, painting landscapes in the country.

Grosz won an international reputation during the 1920s for his savagely satirical pictures. Taking a socialist stance, he mocked the depravity of the ruling classes, which he contrasted with the distress of the poor. Grosz fled to the USA when the Nazis came to power, but never settled happily there.

Metropolis (1916-17), by Grosz. This early work by Grosz, painted in his 20s, shows the influence of Cubist, Futurist and Expressionist art. It was one of a series of paintings depicting a nightmarish vision of life in the Metropolis (the big city, here Berlin), lit in hellish red, with a chaos of people, traffic and buildings crowding in on one another. Later Grosz developed a more personal style, making greater use of his skills of caricature.

Guernica

The most famous of all 20th-century protest paintings is Picasso's *Guernica* (1937). This vast work, nearly 8 metres long, was his response to one of the greatest outrages of the Spanish Civil War. Spanish fascists, led by General Franco, were waging war against the Republican government. In 1937, Franco called on the help of fellow fascists from Germany to launch an air attack on the town of Guernica, in the Basque region of northern Spain. On 26 April, the Germans unleashed the first ever massive air raid on a civilian target, hitting the town on market day. They used new types of aircraft and bombs, and caused nearly 2,000 deaths. The event provoked worldwide condemnation.

That same year, Picasso, still in Paris, was asked by the Republicans to paint a mural for the Spanish pavilion at the Exposition Universelle (World Fair) in Paris.

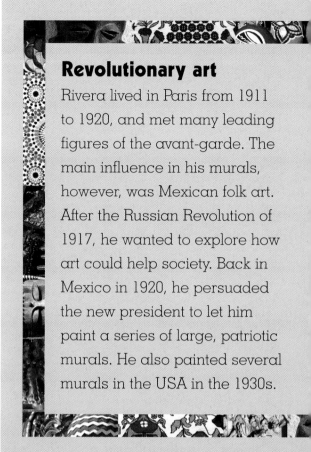

Revolutionary art

Rivera lived in Paris from 1911 to 1920, and met many leading figures of the avant-garde. The main influence in his murals, however, was Mexican folk art. After the Russian Revolution of 1917, he wanted to explore how art could help society. Back in Mexico in 1920, he persuaded the new president to let him paint a series of large, patriotic murals. He also painted several murals in the USA in the 1930s.

Guernica (1937), by Picasso.

Around the World
Mexico

The Mexican Revolution (1910-20) was an uprising that eventually turned Mexico from a dictatorship into a democratic republic. During the instability of the 1920s and 1930s, several artists revived the tradition of mural painting to promote the ideals of the new republic. Diego Rivera (1886-1957) was the most famous of these. A fervent communist, his huge paintings make strong statements about social injustice and the possibilities of a brighter future with socialism.

Copy (1934), by Rivera, of a part of Man at the Crossroads, a mural made for the Rockefeller Center in New York. In a famous controversy, the original was destroyed shortly after completion because it contained so many communist elements.

He chose the bombing of Guernica as his subject, and, driven by rage over the inhuman destruction, he completed the work in just three weeks. Picasso's *Guernica* is like a visual howl of anguish. Painted in sombre tones – mostly in black and white – it shows the victims of the raid with vivid symbolism: a woman holding a dead baby, a dying horse, the shattered body of a soldier.

During the Second World War (1939-45), a German officer in occupied Paris is said to have visited Picasso in his studio. Seeing a photograph of *Guernica*, the officer asked, "Did you do this?", to which Picasso replied, "No. You did."

Matisse

After the excitement of the Fauve era, Henri Matisse (1869-1954) stepped back from the limelight. Like Picasso, who became a good friend, he worked relentlessly at his art, continually pursuing new themes. His paintings became more tranquil and, after his first visit to Morocco in 1912, suffused with radiant colour. In 1917, now a successful artist with an international reputation, he moved to Nice in the south of France. Here, he began a long series depicting women reclining in Turkish-style dress, which he called Odalisques.

The merits of simplicity

In the 1930s, Matisse's style changed again. It became lighter and freer, with more dynamic drawing and bolder areas of flat colour. He began experimenting with paper cut-outs, using shapes cut from coloured paper. In 1941, aged 71, he had a major operation for cancer. He recovered, but now felt he was living on borrowed time. His work became increasingly experimental. Using cut-outs, he designed highly inventive illustrations for a book, *Jazz*, which was published to great acclaim in 1947.

Matisse continued to work until well into his 80s. Now very frail, he often sat in a wheelchair and made cut-outs, directing an assistant to position them for him. Despite this, he still produced some of his most inventive and joyful work. One of his last works was a large semi-abstract piece called *The Snail* (1953), made out of ten irregular rectangles of coloured paper – a deftly simple example of his mastery of shape, colour and form.

Dance, Grey, Blue, Pink (1935-36), a colour etching by Matisse. Dance was a lifelong theme for Matisse, and he came back to it regularly as his painting evolved. This version is an etching of his large mural, Dance II, a highly stylised work created in 1931-33 for American art collector Alfred Barnes. He designed the piece using paper cut-outs.

Around the World
Morocco

The vibrant colours of Morocco were an important inspiration to Matisse, who made two long trips there in 1912-13. Colour is a key feature of the main art form of Morocco, zillij, or cut-tile mosaics. The skills of the craft have been handed down from generation to generation for hundreds of years.

Tiled fountain at a tomb in Rabat, Morocco.

Enduring splendour

Zillij uses hundreds of specially made glazed pottery tiles of different shapes and sizes. Kiln-baked tiles are arranged in geometric patterns, sometimes of astonishing complexity. They are used to decorate floors and walls in private homes, public buildings, tombs and, above all, mosques. Zillij is very much a living art, but it dates back to the 13th century. Fine examples are also found in southern Spain, which the Moors of North Africa ruled for over 700 years until 1492.

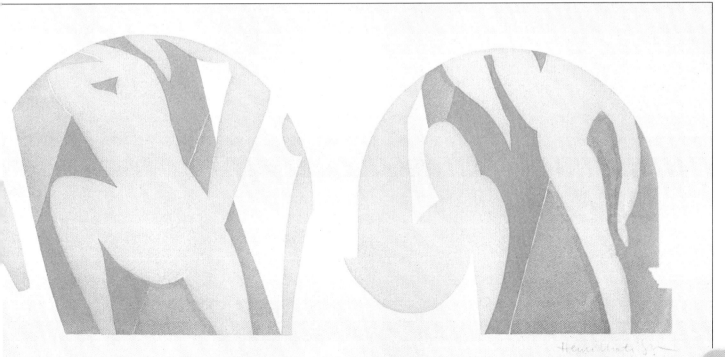

Picasso

Pablo Picasso (1881-1973) was restless, energetic and charismatic to the end of his long life. When he died, aged 91, he was celebrated as the greatest artist of the 20th century. His legacy is hard to assess, as he changed his style so often – in fact, every time he changed his wife or partner, which he did at least seven times. In this respect, his painting is highly autobiographical. His sculpture and constructions were as inventive and influential as his paintings. Perhaps his greatest legacy is the sheer fertility of his imagination; the huge variety of his work has inspired countless artists.

Tireless energy

Picasso abandoned Cubism during the First World War. He married the ballerina Olga Khoklova in 1918, and for a while his painting took a surprising turn towards a traditional, realistic style. But in 1925, he got involved with the Surrealists, and developed a radically new style, with strangely shaped bodies. Thereafter, he often painted grotesque figures and portraits. In the 1930s, he began a large series of etchings and book illustrations, often centring on the themes of bull-fighting and the Minotaur – an image that also appears in *Guernica*.

In Paris during the Second World War, he created sculptures out of objects that he found, such as a bull's head made out of a bicycle saddle and a pair of handlebars (1942). He later had many of his sculptures cast in bronze.

Goat (1950), a sculpture made of plaster, a wicker basket, ceramic pots, palm leaves, metal and wood. This piece is typical of Picasso's playfulness, and his old habit of applying his imaginative invention to found objects. It was later cast in bronze.

After the war, now in his 60s, Picasso moved to the town of Vallauris in the south of France, with his new partner Françoise Gilot and their two babies. In the 1950s, he began to rework various paintings by other artists of the past, such as Velázquez, Delacroix and Manet. For instance, in 1957 he made his own, highly individual versions – 44 in all – of Velázquez's *Las Meninas*. In 1962, he also made cardboard cut-out sculptures based on Manet's *Déjeuner sur l'Herbe*.

Françoise left him in 1953, but he married a second time, aged 79, in 1961. By this time he was world famous and very wealthy. However, he found his fame trying, and hid from the public in a series of grand houses in the south of France. This was the price of fame for a man who had set out to conquer the art world with Cubism some sixty years earlier.

Picasso had no time for abstract art. "There is no abstract art," he declared. "You must always start with something. Afterwards you can remove all traces of reality."

Ceramics

Pottery is one of the oldest art forms on Earth. Many thousands of years ago, people found that solid utensils could be made by baking shaped clay in a fire, or even better, in an oven, or kiln. Later, they discovered that glass-like glazes could be fused onto the clay in a second firing, making the pottery watertight. The same principles still apply today. The clay itself can be shaped and patterned before firing. Either the glazes can be coloured, or decorative designs can be painted onto the pot using oxides at the glazing stage. This is the technique Picasso used.

Pitcher, with Horse and Rider. Picasso took up ceramics when he moved to the south of France after the Second World War. He worked alongside professional potters in Vallauris. Here he has let his imagination loose on the shape of a traditional pitcher.

Chronology of Art in the Early 20th Century

1893 Munch paints *The Scream*, a key source of inspiration for Expressionism.

1895 Cézanne has his first solo exhibition. His work is a major influence on Fauvism and Cubism.

1897 Beginning of the Vienna Secession.

1900-04 Picasso's Blue Period of painting.

1904-05 Picasso's Rose Period of painting.

1905 Fauvism is launched in Paris. Die Brücke is formed in Dresden.

1907 Picasso paints *Les Demoiselles d'Avignon*.

1908 Cubism is launched in Paris.

1909 The *Futurist Manifesto* is published in Paris.

1910 Kandinsky produces his first abstract art.

1911 Der Blaue Reiter is formed in Munich. The term Expressionism is coined.

1912 Launch of Orphism (or Orphic Cubism) in Paris.

1914 Outbreak of the First World War (to 1918).

1915 Malevich founds Suprematism in Russia.

1916 Dada begins at the Cabaret Voltaire, Zürich.

1917 The Russian Revolution. Beginning of Constructivism in Russia. Mondrian launches De Stijl in The Netherlands.

1924 Publication of the *Surrealist Manifesto* in Paris.

1925 Neue Sachlichkeit (New Objectivity) is founded in Germany. Art Deco emerges in Paris.

1926 Death of the last Impressionist, Monet.

1933 The Nazis come to power in Germany.

1936 Outbreak of the Spanish Civil War (to 1939).

1937 Picasso paints *Guernica*. The Nazis show their hatred of the avant-garde with a display of 'Degenerate Art', mocking work by Picasso, Mondrian, Kandinsky, Grosz, Dix and others.

1939 Outbreak of the Second World War (to 1945).

1954 Death of Matisse.

1973 Death of Picasso.

A Brief History of Art

The earliest known works of art are small, carved figurines dating from 30,000 BC. Cave painting dates back to 16,000 BC. Sculpture was the great art form of Ancient Greece, from about 500 BC. Greek sculptors made brilliantly lifelike images.

In Europe, the Renaissance began in the 1300s, when artists in Italy rediscovered the culture of the ancient Romans and Greeks. Renaissance artists include painters such as **Giotto** (c.1267-1337), **Leonardo da Vinci** (1452-1519), and **Jan van Eyck** (c.1390-1441). **Michelangelo Buonarroti** (1475-1564) made sculpture as fine as the Romans or Greeks had produced.

In Europe, Mannerist painters such as **El Greco** (1541-1614) were putting emotion into their paintings. Baroque painters such as **Pieter-Paul Rubens** (1577-1640) displayed dazzling technical skill and a sense of glamour. The Dutch painter **Rembrandt van Rijn** (1606-69) showed in his portraits how painting could capture the sitter's character.

Artists now painted detailed pictures of reality, but this was not enough any more. Painters like **Francisco Goya** (1746-1828) adapted their style to convey expression and emotion. Emotion was a key element of Romanticism. In his late work, **JMW Turner** (1775-1851) used dashes of colour to convey feeling.

In the Realist movement, artists like **Gustave Courbet** (1819-77) used their skills to portray real life. In the 1870s, Impressionists such as **Pierre-Auguste Renoir** (1841-1919) and **Claude Monet** (1840-1926) took Realism in a new direction. They painted outdoors, and rapidly, trying to capture the passing moments of the world. Post-Impressionists such as **Paul Gauguin** (1848-1903), **Vincent van Gogh** (1853-90) and **Paul Cézanne** (1839-1906) developed highly individual styles.

In the 20th century, a series of movements followed each other. In Cubism, **Pablo Picasso** (1881-1973) explored new ways to look at objects. Expressionism concentrated on putting emotion into painting. The Surrealists, such as **Salvador Dalí** (1904-89) and **René Magritte** (1898-1967), depicted imaginative, dreamlike worlds. The development of abstract art was taken a step further in the works of **Piet Mondrian** (1872-1944), while **Jackson Pollock** (1912-56) launched Abstract Expressionism. In the late 20th century, Pop artists like **Andy Warhol** (1928-87) explored the meaning of art, as did Minimalists such as **Carl Andre** (1935-). Installation artists such as **Joseph Beuys** (1921-86) took art in new directions.

Glossary

Abstract art
Any form of art that does not represent things in the real world, but is composed simply of shapes or colours.

Academic art
A formal, traditional and highly polished kind of painting, as taught and promoted by the official schools of painting, called academies.

Avant-garde
The leaders of new trends in art – those ahead of public taste. The term is from the French for vanguard (soldiers at the head of an army).

Collage
The technique of creating images by selecting, cutting out and sticking down bits of paper and other printed material.

Complementary colours
Colours that appear on the opposite sides of a colour wheel, in which one primary colour (red, yellow or blue) faces a mixture of the other two. Complementary colours intensify each other when placed side by side.

Divisionism
A technique like Pointillism, using dots of unmixed colour to build up a picture.

Naive art
Art that looks as though it might have been done by a child or an untrained artist.

Photomontage
A way of building up an image using cut-out photos – a technique developed by the Dadaists.

Index